Screwed Up:
Penitentiary Poetry

Screwed Up: Penitentiary Poetry

Screwed Up:
Penitentiary Poetry

Compiled by
Cory Kaufmann

Self-Published

ISBN: 9798778122758

Edited by Justin Monahan, Harley Kaufmann-Sacrey, and Rebecca
Riley.

Contributions by Jessica Riley.

Illustrations and cover design by Allie Lafleur.

Self-Published by Cory Kaufmann.

Follow us on Instagram:
@pentuppoems

Some people
are not capable of change,
and some are

Screwed Up: Penitentiary Poetry is a collection of poems written, compiled, and self-published exclusively by long-term federal prisoners - a first of its kind.

Our reality is a constant state of letdowns, disappointments, and loss of control. This poetry in this collection is our outlet to voice our emotions, while living in a space where voicing our emotions may not be so welcome.

The release of this book has tremendous significance - not only on a personal level for myself and the authors, but also in that it represents a glimmer of autonomy in a place where we have none. As the compiler, I have difficulty putting it into words how impactful this book is, as it represents more than just my interaction with incarceration. I have found, through my experiences in the multiple systems that I have been moved in and out of, a feeling of connection between myself and my fellow inmates.

Imagine every single goal you are working towards comes to a grinding halt. Imagine all your wildest dreams turning into your worst nightmares. Imagine all your hopes fading away, to be put on a shelf for at least 15 years. This book represents a motion to make these goals, dreams, and hopes come back to life and seem more tangible. It gives hope to the hopeless, and goals to those with no direction. By reading this, you are supporting a human trying to get their life back on track.

I am not trying to garner sympathy from you, nor am I trying to gain your empathy; none of the authors are. We know that our actions have consequences, and we fully accept them. All I ask is that you remember that some of us are truly capable of change and are not bad people. We made a bad decision during a challenging time in our lives.

On that note, it is important to express to our readers that these authors are all remorseful and regretful for their actions, and more importantly, conduct themselves in a manner which reflects that.

All the names in this book are pseudonyms, however each author is credited for their contribution to this book.

Lastly, to give this book some life, included is a list of all the penitentiaries where these poems were conceived and written:

- Millhaven Institution, Bath, On.
- Kingston Penitentiary (KP), Kingston, On.
- Edmonton Institution, Edmonton, Ab.
- Joyceville Institution, Kingston, On.
- Fenbrook Institution, Gravenhurst, On.
- Stony Mountain Institution, Winnipeg, Mb.
- Beaver Creek Institution, Gravenhurst, On.
- Warkworth Institution, Campbellford, On.
- Frontenac Institution, Kingston, On.
- Rockwood Institution, Winnipeg, Mb.
- Regional Treatment Centre, Bath, On.
- Regional Psychiatric Centre, Saskatoon, Sk.

Please enjoy this collection of poetry from people working to reclaim their hopes and dreams.

Contents

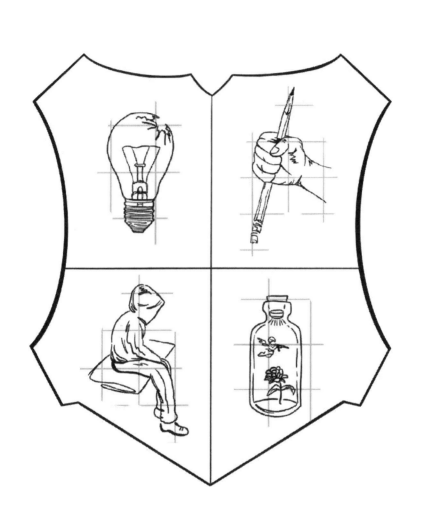

The following poetry is written by:

W. T. W.

One More Chance

Love, please forgive me.
I've let you down in the past,
For I was young and foolish.
Now, I need something that will last.

Yesterday, you were just a game,
And I was wild and free,
Not knowing of your power,
Only now it is plain to see.

The years have past
And the days slip slowly by.
Now my heart aches,
For your love, it cries.

So love bless me one more chance.
Please say it's not too late,
Only you can save...
This lonely heart, it's fate.

-April 1988

"Dedicated to *Sarah when she was in England and I didn't know if she'd ever come back to Canada."

*Name has been changed to protect privacy

A Truer Heart Than Mine

Your heart was truer than mine could be,
That's why I'm lonesome today.
You tried your best to hold on to me,
But somehow I slipped away.
I doubted my love and showed it so,
And I will always regret that day.
I want you and the rest of the world to know,
That I deserve to pay.

I can only say, "I'm sorry now!"
Please forgive my foolish heart,
For breaking every promised vow,
That made us drift apart.

I know that I have lost you,
But please, in the heart, somehow,
Forgive me all that I've cost you.

That's all I am asking now!

        -1988

"Dedicated to my partner after I was convicted and I didn't think I'd ever see her again."

Cheer Up

I know the time, that seems so hard
Can make life seem so wasted,
But when you're down, just think of all,
The things untouched or tasted.
Think of things you haven't done,
And all you want to do.
Flying or driving or swinging from trees,
If that will help you through.
But of all the things you shouldn't do,
I think this is the worst,
It's feeling sorry for yourself,
Cuz you know you'll only burst!
Better to think of me, and the way that I,
Could always make you giggle.
Think of a chick with a nice tight ass,
And the cutest little wiggle!
Think of her p**** on your face,
or riding on your c***.
And pound your PUD and fantasize,
And blow it in your sock.
Whatever you do, just don't get down
And think of a great big castle,
I'm telling ya now, ya better listen
And f*****' cheer up asshole!!

-Christmas 1988

"KP was often a miserable place, with wall-to-wall anger and attitude, but my buddy Derrick was always in a good mood and ready with a joke to make you smile."

"Before my friend was released from KP he gifted this to me for Xmas, every time I read it I still giggle and laugh and remember what a great friend he was."

My Best Friend

You made me laugh
When I wanted to cry
You even wiped the tears
From my eyes.

You picked me up
 when I was feeling blue,
And you stood by me,
When I needed you
Because not many would do.

So it doesn't matter what you do
Or where in life you go,
You'll always be my best friend,
It's something I thought you should know.

-June 1988

To sit behind these dreary walls is really quite unreal.
But the loneliness that we all know I think you also feel.
To be behind these iron bars, is not where I want to be.
But to be let out to run about
To feel that we are free. but soon, one day, I'll be let out
Oh please, do not say never,
I will tell you this, I hope you know, they can't keep me here
forever.

-1990

Requiem for a Friend

MY DEAR FAUX
I NEVER REALLY REALIZED,
I NEVER WAS AWAKE,
HOW THE WORLD LOOKED SO MUCH BETTER,
JUST BECAUSE YOU WERE THERE.

IT'S FUNNY HOW THINGS JUST HAPPEN,
CHANCE MEETINGS CHANGE OUR LIVES,
NEW MEANINGS, NEW BEGINNINGS,
NEW HOPE'S IN NEW ALLIES.

BUT JUST AS FATE HAS GIVEN,
FATE DECIDES TO TAKE AWAY,
LEAVING WONDER, PAIN, DAMNATION,
STILL... REALIZATION RULES THE DAY.

YOU'VE LEFT A MARK, OH DEAREST FRIEND,
TIME OR ACTIONS CANNOT ERASE,
YOU SET OUR SOULS AND SPIRITS FREE,
AND BLESSED OUR EARTHLY DAYS.

BUT NOW I PASSED THROUGH DAY-TO-DAY,
SEARCHING FOR SOMETHING LOST.
AND YET, DEEP DOWN, I KNOW WHAT'S MISSING,
AND THE PAIN SHOWS HOW MUCH IT COST.

AND SO, DEAR FAUX, "HOW'S IT GOING EH?"
"A LOT BETTER THAN YESTERDAY!" YOU JEST.
SO FINALLY I HAVE TO SAY, DEAR FRIEND,

YOU WERE AND ARE THE BEST,

-May 1990

"He was afraid to be deported back to his native Grenada in 1990… I was told he had died, murdered, two days after his arrival home.

R.I.P. MY BROTHER"

"I remember to read this every August 10th as a tribute to my friend."

Autumn Grace

As I sit out and look at the trees,
I long to feel the softness of the autumn breeze.
From morn to night I can't resist
The beauty that lies beyond the velvety crests,
The radiant sun that shines among the tress,
Gives beauty to the different colours of the leaves,
The birds that fly and sing so merrily,
Bring much joy and tranquility to me,
Autumn is a time that I love best,
It takes me away from my strife and unrest,
Of my life's difficulties and regrets,
It gives me peace and happiness.
With the autumn crimson of the leaves,
And the soft blowing of the breeze,
Brings nature blooming at it's best,
And makes me think how we are blessed,
And how I wish to be free of this mess.

-Fall 1988

"My first Autumn in prison, and missing so much the start of hockey and football seasons"

Confronting the Beast

These foolish fears
That frighten me so
That have led me emotionally astray.

In confusion they seek
The ones that are weak
And finds a mind to pray.

They nibble and chew
Destroying most pleasures
From the fruits of my mind
They will feast

There's no escape…
This self-torturing hate.
Beware the stalking of the beast.

One moment they're gone
You catch your breath
Your suffering has just begun.

In your mind they will creep
Even when you're asleep
There's nowhere you can run.

Beware the stalking of the beast.

-1991

Behind These Walls

Behind These Walls
The man tell tales
Of lives destroyed
And futures derailed.

The weak old Men
In their battered clothes
Told stories
For the Young
And even the old.

But when they were done
They returned to their cells
Not knowing they were living
...and already in hell.

-1991

My Surroundings...

The days pass slowly in this living hell,
All emotions of good are lost,
Hatred and anger swell.

Cold, thin air carries along
The stench of Broken Spirits,
The Souls of those lost inside,
This steel maze.

No songs are sung,
No kind words are spoken,
Eyes stare out of nameless faces,
The burning fires of the Mad,
The scared,
The angry.

In the night there are screams of Minds blown apart.

The final Futile beat before the Silence of the heart.

-1991

*"EVIL DEEDS LIKE VILE WEEDS
BLOOM WELL IN PRISON AIR.
IT IS ONLY WHAT IS GOOD IN MEN
THAT WASTES AND WITHERS THERE."***

*-Oscar Wilde (while he was in READING
GAOL)*
***"An inspirational quote I have always been
conscious of."*

*"3 years at Kingston Pen and I was becoming
all too aware of how the place was starting to
affect me... and others."*

My Loss

In the dawning light
I gaze into your eyes
And try to comprehend
The wards I wish were lies.

I try to close my ears
As you speak of someone new
One who's stolen your heart
While you're breaking mine in two.

As you bid me farewell
In a voice that cracks with pain
I stand and watch you go
And I fall apart again.

I don't call out to stop you
There are no words to say
The tears roll down my cheeks
For all I've lost today.

-January 1994

"Just days before *Sarah went back to England and I'd never see her again."

"We were together 9 years, 6 of which I spent in prison, before she had enough of being alone so far from her home."

I feel the pain almost every day.
I can't forget her,
There's just no way.

My feelings for her,
Will last forever,
Until the time,
We are back together.

And if it happens,
That we don't meet,
I'll remember her always
'Cause she can't be beat!

-Fall 1994

"Months after *Sarah left me, and I'd heard that she married someone in England."

Time is On Our Side

Time is on our side,
Till the ends of the earth I will chase you,
Till I once again can embrace you,
To hold you close,
To hold me near,
To caress you, and whisper sweet lovings in my ear.

A kiss on the neck…
A shudder of ecstasy…
A passion so strong…

You will live inside me forever,
And take away our fears.

Time is on our side.

-By *Sarah, July 1995

"Received at Warkworth, 17 months after she left me and returned to her native England – 10 months after she married a guy she knew in her teen years."

"I received this in a birthday card with a sexy Polaroid photo I was allowed to see but not keep!"

"There has been no other contact between us, as of Sept. 2021."

What comes next?
I have no idea.
Everyday brings a new pain,
The memories are enemies.
It's been years
Since she disappeared
But she's still here,
Living in a memory.
She whispers in my ear.
A silent souvenir,
And I taste a tear.
My memories are enemies.

-2000

"6 years after my wife and son left Canada."

Today...

I was reminded of you...
Taken back to a special place in time...

And as I thought of you
A certain sort of sadness
Filled my heart...

Even though the memories we have
Are beautiful, like you...
And thinking back on them,
Fills my heart with joy,
My eyes also swell with tears,
Because we are still,
So many years and still,
So far apart.

And I miss you very much...

...today.

-2004

"10 years after *Sarah left me and went back to England."

For No Reason

Sometimes I'm surprised,
To find how much you're still with me.

How easily my mind finds you,
In searching for a place to rest.

It seems that somewhere,
In the years and oceans in between us,
The thought of you should have faded...

But no,
At the slightest reason-

Indeed,
For no reason at all-

I think of you!

-2004

Life…

Has new meaning now
As my day begins,

I'm learning to let go of,
Mine and other's sins.

With new understanding,
Patience and trust,

I'm looking inside now,
To see as I must.

Out of my confusion,
Bit by bit.

The pieces of my puzzle
Are starting to fit.

-2016

It Must Be...

What is it man can never buy?
Some people must be shown.

What is it that he cannot steal,
Or rent, or lease to own?

And what is it, you only get,
When you decide to give?

And why is it, this feeling that
I speak of makes you live?

It also hurts and makes you cry,
It also makes you fear.

It makes you wish and hope and pray,
By day, week, month, and year.

This feeling that we should know,
The one I'm writing of.

I guess by now, you all have guessed,
Of course, it must be love.

-2016

"After years of reconciliation and self-examination, I embraced my spirituality and truly began to feel The Love of God."

The following poetry is written by:

AB

DANCE OF THE BLACK MAMBA

PIPE UP THE CHARMER'S FLUTE,
BEAT THE GOAT SKIN DRUM.
COME CLOSER TO YOUR PREY, AFRICA.
SEE YOUR LOVER COMING; THE PLANE HAS LANDED.

NO, OH NO, WE DON'T WALTZ OR TANGO
IN AFRICA, WE DO THE SHANGO.
INTOXICATING IS THE RHYTHUM,
FEEL YOUR BODY AS IT SWAYS TO THE DRUM.

HYPNOTIC IS ITS BEAUTY;
ENCHANTED IS THE BEAST.
YOU'RE AT HOME IN AFRICA
ENJOY THE FEAST.

CHARMED BY ITS GRACE;
LIKE THE BLACK MAMBA,
YOU'RE AT HOME IN THIS PLACE.
DANCE THE DANCE OF LOVERS,
SWAY TO ITS SWEET ECSTASY,
LIVE THE DREAM FULFILL THE FANTASY.

AS THE TREES SWAY IN THE OPEN AIR,
TO THE RHYTHM ALL THEIR OWN,
AND THE MIGHTY LION ROAR (SIMBA),
ENJOY YOUR STAY IN AFRICA AND DANCE THE DANCE
OF THE BLACK MAMBA.

-08/12/12

LOVE LETTERS

LOVE LETTERS STRAIGHT FROM THE HEART,
KEEPS US TOGETHER THOUGH WE ARE FAR APART.
I HEAR YOUR VOICE THROUGH THE WHISPER OF AIR,
A BREADTH OF PERFUME LINGERS THERE, I SEARCH
FOR YOU ONLY TO FIND,
I WAS DEEP ASLEEP WITH YOU ON MY MIND.
I HAVE GOT TO REALIZE I AM DOING TIME. YES AND
TIME WILL HEAL THE PAIN, FOR WE WILL BE TOGETHER
SOON AGAIN. BUT WHENEVER I AM FEELING
DOWN AND BLUE
ANOTHER LOVE LETTER I WILL WRITE TO YOU.

JOURNEY

WHERE ARE YOU GOING?
TO CLIMB THE HOLY MOUNTAIN.
WHERE ARE YOU GOING?
TO DRINK FROM THE SPIRITUAL FOUNTAIN.
WHERE ARE YOU GOING?
TO CROSS THE OPEN SEA.
WHERE ARE YOU GOING?
TO A PLACE I CAN BE FREE.
WHERE ARE YOU GOING?
TO HEAR THE TRUMPET SOUND.
WHERE ARE YOU GOING?
TO WATCH PEOPLE DANCE AROUND.
WHERE ARE YOU GOING?
TO STAND IN A LINE.
WHERE ARE YOU GOING?
TO MEET THE MOST DIVINE.
WHERE ARE YOU GOING?
TO EAT BREAD AND HONEY.
WHERE ARE YOU GOING?
TOWARDS A HIGHER JOURNEY.
DO YOU KNOW WHERE YOU ARE GOING.
IT'S NEVER TOO LATE TO STOP AND CHOOSE ANOTHER
JOURNEY.

ENRAGED

ENRAGED! ENCAGED!
LOCKED AWAY FROM SOCIETY,
I MUST HAVE MISSBEHAVED OR DID I?
AM I A VICTIM OR A PERPETRATOR?
THAT DEPENDS ON WHOM YOU ASK.
A SOCIATIAL MISFIT, OR JUST A CONVICT,
A MAN WITH A PURPOSE
I JUST HAVEN'T FOUND MY NICHE,
A LANE OF MY OWN A PLACE TO CALL HOME.
FREEDOM IS JUST AN ILLUSION
FOR ONE CAUGHT IN HIS OWN PRISON.
ENRAGED! ENCAGED!
SO YOU LOOK DOWN ON ME SAY I'LL NEVER BE FREE,
BUT WHO ARE YOU?
JUST ANOTHER FOOL WHO DOSEN'T EVEN REALIZE
YOU'RE ENRAGED! YOUR ENCAGED!
IN A WORLD OF DELUSION,
NO ONE MAN IS BETTER THAN ANY OTHER FOR WE ARE
ALL ENRAGED, ALL ENCAGED.

MY BLACK IDENTITY

BLACK I AM
BLACK I AM PROUD TO BE.
NO ONE CAN ROB ME OF MY BLACK IDENTITY.
HERE I SIT IN A WORLD, THAT'S AFRAID OF ME,
BECAUSE OF OUR BLACK HISTORY.
I AM A MAN OF INTELLIGENCE,
WHICH I AM NOT SUPPOSED TO BE!
ALL BECAUSE I WAS BORN WITH A BLACK IDENTITY.
AM I JUST A SKIN COLOR? OR SO IT MAY SEEM TO ME,
ALL DUE TO MY BLACK IDENTITY,
FOREVER HAVING TO PROVE YOURSELF, YOU'RE NOT
SUPPOSED TO BE SMART, ARTICULATE, HANDSOME OR
BEAUTIFUL.
THAT'S THE STRUGGLE OF A PERSON WITH A BLACK
IDENTITY AND A PURE HEART.
IS NOT JUSTICE SUPPOSED TO BE BLIND,
YET WE ARE FOREVER JUDGED ON OUR BLACK
IDENTITY.
AND ALWAYS REFERED TO AS A VISIBLE MINORITY.
THAT'S WHY
I AM PROUD OF MY BLACK IDENTITY.

ODE TO A GANGSTER

YOU LIVED SO FAST,
YOU DIED SO YOUNG;
FOR THE KIDS YOU LEFT BEHIND,
I HAVE TO BE STRONG.
WE MADE A PROMISE TO EACH OTHER,
FOREVER YOU WILL BE MY BROTHER.
THE PAIN IS DEEP,
THE GRIEF IS LONG
I GOT TO FIND A WAY TO STAY STRONG.
I'LL ALWAYS REMEMBER YOU IN A SONG.
THE ONE WE PLAYED IN THE HOOD.
DURING THE DAYS,
WHEN WE WERE UP TO NO GOOD,
NOW YOU ARE GONE,
ANOTHER O.G. ORIGINAL GANGSTER THAT IS,
GONE TO SOON,
UP THERE IN HEAVEN BRIGHT SHINING AS
THE MOON.
YOU WILL NEVER BE FORGOTTEN! NIGGA,
YOU ARE FOREVER ENSHRINED IN,
AN ODE TO A GANGSTER R.I.P.

The following poetry is written by:

Cory Kaufmann

One To

Just want one to not judge me.
Just want one to want to hug me.
Just want one to want me as myself.
Just want one to be herself.
Just want one to really need me.
Just want one to not be too needy.
Just want one to love me like no other.
Just want one to be the perfect lover.

-August 2021

The following poetry is written by:

Mountain River Valley

imagine a man
        wandering in the driest of deserts
where all life crouches in quiet suffering
        under a burning sun.
              all is emptiness...
              the sky,
                    the horizon...
the ground beneath his feet,
        the barest of stones,
              the smallest grains of sand.
all is silent.
not even a breath to whisper life.

and in this desolation,
        in his sorrow, with neck bowed
              beneath the weight of loneliness
he kneels to weep,

        his tears
tracing the contours of his face
        to fall upon motionless

and with his eyes closed he prays
and waits for something, for anything,
to remind him of life as it was before this waste.

he lays to sleep, perchance to dream
and wakes as one swimming up from great depths
to see before his eyes a scarlet splash.
a few small green leaves
        a flower
from his tears.

        -may 19, 2016
        the desert lives.

words scattered about like yesterday's seeds?
       see which take root and flourish?
          carefully chose to nourish?
               wait to see the blossoms bloom?
and in picking eat the fruit
and be nourished in return?

to stand within the garden mother makes
and see the beauty and the love...
the strength to withstand the torrential rain
and greet the sun again
with the smiling face of God's good grace?

to know the gifts a mother gives
flow river-like through each day
       and try to pass them on
          to all we touch
             in each and every
                way.

Do not throw those seeds away!

    -17-2-17

words scattered about
like yesterday's seed,
flourish in love's garden.
tell me, Mary.
            how does your garden grow?
            such delight-filled flowers
                        all in a row.

there is one birthday i shall never forget.
even though i forget my own sometime,
there is one birthday i shall never forget.

this day in which the birthday lives
is filled with tender memories
of cool hands upon a fevered brow
and a gentle voice in a world of pain.
of love and care i had my share
and more than enough it was,
to tend life's wounds and bring me joy
and quiet tea amid a busy afternoon.

when pressed for gift requests
her usual reply did not suffice
and after asking thrice she finally
gave voice...

            a poem...

                        and a hand-made card
                        was all she asked.

                        so, a poem she has won.
for this, this poem is done.

and now i need to find my box

of coloured wicks,

some paper,

and some glue.

...i think some reds and shades of blue
        for her garden flowers do.

        -2017-4-14
        For my mother
        On her 85th birthday.

do you dare to stand just there
weaving sunlight in your hair
shadowed limbs in flowered air
beauty personified
some sweet forgotten pair
laughing at some forgotten fair

do you dare to just stand there
upon the speckled stair
with freckles dancing in frosted cream
and leave me feeling lost
within some summer's dream?

winter's wind cannot touch me nor
bring me down
when remembering how,
with roses heavenly scent
i first saw you
standing suspended upon the stair.

the universe within your eye
full and round within love's warm
embrace.
dappled sun upon the wonder of your face.

-17-6-15

i knew a man who cried at sunsets
and baby birds fallen from the nest.
        some said he was depressed
        but I knew he grew
                taller
        while he slept.

i knew a man who danced each step.
some said he was possessed.
but I knew he had regressed
beyond obsessed.
he was just a shout short of
        ole.

i knew a womyn once
who taught me how to be free
even when oppressed.
she gave me books to read
and showed me the follies of reason.

i met a child
who grew up to be
        me.
don't you see?

        -17-7-3
        for the moment.

61

it isn't easy being beautiful.
to find one's self physically attractive,
like some magnet to strange creatures
who want to own you,
or break you because beauty somehow
threatens them.
and god forgive the idolaters
who want to place you
high upon the pedestal of their adoration,
which later turns out
to hold only the isolation any collected thing suffers
at the hands of those who do not understand
love is more than some empty gesture.

there is more love in the finger of a fly
than joy upon the morrow,
when awakening to the knowing
it's not understanding you have found
but possession by another.

the wrapping may be part of the gift
but life is so much richer
if we are more than just the child
distracted by the bow.

    -17/9/14
    For Jackie
    & her treasures within.

fart boogie noodles spill across the floor
like sparkling new wine and jailhouse macaroni.
the masked womyn unveils and delightful laughter
cuts like a newly sharpened knife
where only silence reigned before.

shadows rise before floodlights
and the pause before the clapper snaps
doesn't have time to brood.

with a toss to the left and a nod to the right
the audience is forewarned...
here comes the chameleon to perform.

voices drawn from imagined within
speak across the gathered heads
to ring against the echoing wall,
and time is cast back to greet
the lady and her beau,
who, having been called beyond himself,
finds a new tongue with which to call
to the ghosts of actors past.

bow to the magic of theatre.
the cauldron's power...
the mixing disparate parts
to find the united whole,
sweeping together into
a new gathering of one.
experience the mysterious rites
of art and her performing wonder

oh suppose she was only womyn
and miss the moment's truth.

the lady's muse has melded and fused
life into the fleeting.

to her I offer my most precious.
to her I rejoice in the gift of her presence
and give thanks.
to her I give
…my Scoobie Do underwear.

-17-9-25
for Claire
and Scoobie Do underwear.

Seagull cries endless,
To anyone who will listen,
Feed me fish not pears.

Small spud are yum yum
Big spuds go by the gum gum
But yams are just dum.

Distant mountain haze
Speaks of fire and fir and risk
Of birds without homes.

Green apples and spam
Like red ketchup on hot dogs
Make me unhappy.

Cars fast too long gone
Are like fish that fly on songs
Flashing splash says the end.

Purple visions dance
Round rooms without corners spin
Squares without chance prance.

-17-9-29

regret, like happiness
 is fleeting.
in the moment only
Joy.

split the infinite and
find only the moment.

imagination and creation
are one.

timeless floating within
Eternity.

connected by space
the notes of the song,
that is life,
are not-song
but a sing-a-long.

more than boundaries.
more than the sand
the line is drawn upon.
more than the ocean's kiss
upon my mother's bones.
more than the moons of jupiter.
more than the galaxy.
more than the milky way.
more than the sound of silence.
more than the still mind.
i just wish the part of me that is
the asian in the yellow sea
would quit eating the part of me
that is the sea urchin.

it keeps giving the me that is
the pampa cows of argentina
...gas.

-17-11-2

touching the chi leaves me
breathless and full
of bees buzzing throughout my body.

my body lifts my mood
like water floats a boat.

winds whip water into waves
that crash upon the shore.

the tree rooted drinks deep
from within the earth's embrace.

falling leaf soars and swooping
brushes against the winter grasses.

business mouse pauses to watch
clouds fly high above the clearing sky,
and touches nose to tail to circle to life
lived simply
within the love of creation.

-17-11-10

dancing bears are people too.

within the ordered routine of a canadian prison
chaos raises its ugly head
and stirs from its restless bed

who said the play's the thing?

actors upon the stage recite prose and poetry
and broken lyrics from some forgotten song

in the audience sits a novice...
writer...
curse of those trying to portray
scenes from another day
within the theatre's domain.

where's the trained eye of the critic
art?

lost to the world
the gestures expressed for better or worse.

hopes are dashed upon the rocks of callous misfortune.

but lo...
raised upon the branches of leviathan tree,
the mighty spoken word prevails
and the fingered pen
has written
and moved on.

in back alleys the young recite lines
a thousand years old.

the cats sing and the dogs howl
and in the far off back someone yowls
and the acid comment etches new faces
with the desire to tell stories seven ages old.

yowling critics don't die...
they grow yellow and old
like the pages foretold...

and just fade away.

-17-12-12
a christmas noel.

there was a stranger came
bearing an enormous bag of maple leaves.
he sat upon them on the corner of fourth and main.
passersby would curiously glance at them
out of the sides of withdrawn eyes.

the demanding would ask him why the leaves.
and he would lament the dying presses of print media
or discuss the dearth of wool and the lack of lamb
in the public diet.

those giving more than just their lips to the service
of the needy
might inquire while offering a cup of coffee
what use a man without a garden might need of leaves
and he would speak of the greenery between the scenery
of the concrete city.

only a very few might hear how he always wanted
a chair of beans to recline upon in his retirement
but couldn't refuse the mice who asked for just one,
or two,
for supper.

but only he truly knew
the dreams their scents brought to his nights.
of forest groves of ancient beings rejoicing
in the communion of their roots.
of standing people swaying in moonlight breezes
while others gave thanks for the gifts the trees
showered upon them.
of earthen sky and fungal fruits,
of growth and decay and growth again.

if you are quiet in your approach
to the corner of fourth and main
you might just see a bag of leaves
and a man within it,
his bearded head just peeking forth
with gentle smile
and softly snoring voice.

      -17-12-27
      for the old man in the forest

potato nipples
                      nibble & sprout fuschia
                 burgundy cosmo-licious areolas

standing tall with wishes to be kissed...
                    & fuzzy bees bless them with
               noses pressed against their needy centers.

and sunflowers shout, "look look, look at me
          i'm so tall and free, look at me."   and who
cannot?

and shy chamomile
                  with her petals slumped like the pale
arms of wallflowers in gymnasiums everywhere
        holds

        her secret fragrance tight till tickled by the touch light
& love's mature & heady scent proclaims the promise
                       of buckwheat's honeyed
                       compliment...
       nectar for the night.

oh kiss potato's honeyed lips & and breathe deep the   scented
night & at
                  last
tongue the nippled being
           satisfied   to sleep contented dreams.

      -18-9-6
      for penelope's button.

lately the dreams of kisses will not let me be
soft and whispery the lips brush back the tears (years) warm and
welcoming the ripe fullness greeting home
hard and heavy the searching hunger

kisses fall like summer's rain

sizzling like bacon singing before the eggs fall

kisses light upon winter's chilly cheek

kisses full of laughter and bubbling bright along my chin.

surprises in the night simply primal
and so easily met

kisses for the lips and thigh

kisses for the long goodbye

lately the dreams of kisses will not let me be.

    -18-9-28

womyn of my dreams
playful, witty, wise
laughing, teasing, expectant
of my will to follow
the teachings they give me
as a slalom past the gates
of this cultural programming
mess the collective someones
have created.
skiing free between the cliff's edge
and the forest of trees, chanting
"bees knees, bees knees, bees knees",
and I don't even know which one of
those funny ladies, those dream-walking,
slow-talking, fast-dancing
peace-filled
spirits
whispered this whiskered mantra
in my one good dreaming ear
or what it is I'm supposed to learn from it.

I just hope the slope doesn't end with a leap into the unknown.
I really don't want to have to learn how to fly
in this bunny suit.

-the fall of 2018

there is upon some distant shore a maid
                    Mary Anne
who keeps a garden as before.

with one eye upon the weather
the other gazes upon her charges'
deepening slumber.
soon winter's blanket will guard them from
Jack Frost's hoary bite
and leave them to the starry night.

the earth's worm burrows deep
and the groundhogs curl their tiny feet
beneath the roots of summer.

the squirrels have dug their last till spring's thaw
frees their treasures from winter's cast.

does the maid seek the merry fiddle's music?
or settle into some chair's comforting embrace
before a fire's flickering face...
to discover life's creative voice
upon the written page?

or does the palette of another
stir within the use of colour
and the garden's splendour
                remembered
grace the world around her?

            -18-11-2
            for the maid Mary Anne.

womyn on the bench
       dewey earth scents
after a long time without rain
sunbeams kaleidoscope sky
clouds hanging high
above the rustling trees
robin sings daylight's ebb
contented pools of peace
settle upon the evening's air
and summer's calm
is memory

-Aug 20, 2019

don't you smile (at me)
       I can't be weak-kneed and still be able to walk away (from
you).
you don't want me
I can't stay
don't you smile at me
       I've got to be on my way.

oh you've been hurt before
       I get it don't you know
someone's ruint it for me
and I won't get to show
I'm not the other fella.
it's not me that's got to let go.
so don't you smile at me.

I'm no romeo.
being too...
don't confuse me with some lothario.
I've got lumbago.
and I've got to go.

+++++++++++++++++++++++++++++++

give me a girl with country
under her fingernails,
been known to find her pigtails
on the rear end of a ham,
and ain't afraid to slam her door
in the face of a man too
fresh for the pan.

give me a girl with country
on the soles of her feet

and the fresh-dipped smell
of a river's walk.

give me a girl with country
singing in her ears,
knowing how the squirrels squawk
when raking up their acorns and their leaves.

give me a girl with country…
I like to hear her talk
and see her walk...
even if it's away from me.

-Sept. 3/19

come sit beside me
and tell me your tale.
I've admired you from afar
and now here you are,
full of light and
       focused like an old guitar,
ringing blue and true like a sunny day.
come sit beside (me in your way)
while I listen to your play (of words).

      stories falling like pennies from heaven
      dance their way down
      through layers of being
      until their meaning sings Tibetan (in a crystal clear night).

(shimmer like a muskoka lake at midnight)

+++++++++++++++++++++++++++++++

are you stuck in an act of resistance?
am I stuck in an act of insistence?
is this a dance for us?

I would rather tumble and fall of the flowing
waters in a northern river
and the beauty in a loon's call as eve comes to rest
like sleep upon a contented breast (-fed babe).
let's not be like two mules
in a tale of...

    -Sept. 3/19

soft sun beams in open windows
while trees whisper themselves in
the rustling breeze.
Rumi whispers cosmic.
St. Theresa nods and graces the moment
with arms spread wide open.

words trigger sweet smells
and the scent of pachuli tickles memories
of beginnings
when flowers were only a thought
and the soup of being moving cellular
danced electric heat
to the beat of far-off fingers snapping.

"oooo", creator said
here comes something...
and it's going to be good.

and some desert heretics,
beatnik beings,
sat in their sweat,
and listened to the wren sing thanks to the world,
and said to themselves... ever so softly...
"ooo", here comes something...
and it's going to be good.
and everywhere laughter stood.

-19/9/4

we look, in the faces of those
we meet,
for the faces of those we loved
when they leave us without saying goodbye.

or our grief, recalled by some
gesture or sign or scent,
visits us anew
and weighs upon us
like some heavy hand
pushing us into solid form
while our spirit shakes
with crying voice.

in my stillness of the moment
respect my silence,
my hesitating, preoccupied depths
of connected loss.
do not worry.
do not fret
at my regret
for the pleasure
at that resemblance
of your ring-tone
to the doorbell
of a former home.

-19-11-17
the surfing grief.

Limericks:

there was a lady from far north
said she didn't give a damn what a penny's worth.
gotta give me more than one dollar
if you think you'll make me holler.
so the gardener gave her a bucket of earth.

*** *** *** ***

had my chance for a loving hug
but thought the girl was going to shrug.
so I didn't go in for the clinch
stepped back and gave an inch
and now her boyfriend's a big mug.

*** *** *** ***

knew a lady grew special flowers.
said they gave her special powers.
So I tried to duck under the pitch
but I couldn't get over the ditch
and now I sit weeding for hours.

*** *** *** ***

here I sit with empty page
like an actor upon a vacant stage.
if only with time
I could find a good line,
I might finish before my old age.

*** *** *** ***

there was a man with a moustache
long enough to wipe a cow's ass.
and he said to the other
that's a mighty fine udder
but I could do without all the green grass.

*** *** *** ***

there was a man tickled pink
who had a rather large rink,
where all the kids from the town
would all gather round,
to watch him skate (rinky-dink) with a mink.

-November 26, 2019

pietro pietro where for art thou,
thy long-haired tonsured monk of long ago?
do you hold your tongue from a place of ire?
or do you care to aspire to a higher place from which to speak?
for who am I, lowly prison-kept stigma
upon the body of our Christ?
or in one are we not the voice of reason-to-be-heard
wherever we raise our voice
to share our pain, our misery inflicted by those who
claim a higher moral ground
only to abuse the trust of others?

scapegoat or beloved goat of God?
how do we know the reception awaiting us upon ascendant climb?
will we be welcomed as beloved child sacrificed
as helpful lessons to instruct others in the folly of belief
in their self-righteous justification of the deconstruction of others?

oh dear brother in meditation
does contemplation's fire
turn to ashes all within?

when they cut the hair from your head
and left only symbolic crown of thorns upon your vessel
did you feel indwelling tide rise to flood your senses?

were you not filled with compassion and understanding?
or did the understanding of the depth of power's corruption
in the body of the cleric bring only tears?
and who did you weep for?

for those lost to siren's song?
or the loss of innocent pretense that you would find sanctuary
from the suffering of ignorance?

only to have it replaced with the suffering of knowing
the wrongs of those claiming to be right?
did you weep for me? or for you?

who do you cry for now?
and where does your spirit wander
that you should visit me in the depth of winter's night
and fill my head
with stories of greedy abbots
and selfish brothers and cloistered sisters?

what good do me your stories of rotten cabbages
and moldy turnips and frozen inks?
of skins scraped holy, translucent and filled with the vanity of
men?
who am I going to share them with?

am I resisting because I cannot see where you want me to go?
or do I resist because I do know and in my knowing faint
to smell cesspools heady scent?

what can you tell me that is not already known by those who care
about the health of embodied earth?
the trick for ghostly voice is to move the conversation to a place
where growth is more than potent seed for spirit's birth.
bring forth the flowers from the hearth.
the facts of life do not always mean we flourish.
bring your wisdom to our dinner
that in supping nourish
and cause amongst us communion's oneness
to settle like downy blanket upon our slumbering form
that we may dream a new creation
suited to a happy planet of new worth
where hearts are deepened with content

to greet the mornings free from lament.
where days are willing spent sharing play
that feeds our needs and shrinks our wants
till all are fed and clean and clothed
and rivers run and wind-blown scent
sings of flowers and children's laughter.

surely brother you can show me mother
who with partner's dance
claims a place with healing touch
that young and old alike do smile
upon the coming night that brings the stars
and calm setting sun
says good light.

      -2019-11-30
      conversing-in-spirit

two ladies came
to cause me pain
like the physiotherapist who said this might twinge
as she gave my foot a flip
and I just passed smooth out
the way the light leaves a room when we flip the switch.

oh I feel better now.
a burden eased.
a little cleaner in spirit.
a little brighter in outlook.
a little happier in memory.

dearly beloved gone
away while I stay behind
to walk a road a little longer
lighter in heart,
with laughter's song
a bird's flight flittering dip
today.

watch and wave goodbye
as two new friends
fade away.

perhaps to meet another day.

-19-12-5

hard headed.

what did it take for me to take dreams seriously?
a lost limb and more aches and pains than you
can shake a stick at.
          hard-headed might just be a
euphemism for dumbass.

i bite my tongue any harder and
i'm going to have to learn sign.

words beg shaping
they whine and snivel
and fill us with drivel
if we listen to the misuse
by others.
words should be like stones
in our pockets...
regretfully thrown, the tossing goodbye
another million years gone
to tell a lover's story.

          -20-3-12

the swallow flitters and skips across the calm.

evening has come to call
        upon the day.

and stillness feels its way
        across the pond.
silent reeds stand tall against the
falling night.

dew kisses the earthen born
        grasses
with lips that taste of honey.

wind-cast seeds float to settle
light upon the waters
        dusty with remembered gravity.

peaceful comes the dark
        across a sky
alive with the lampman's
wandering wand to sparkle bright
the starry lanterns sight.

the fairy stirs the angel's
        loom
to weave upon this day
        this evening's rest.

        -2020-3-12

Life: a trip down a slippery
slope with rollerblades
and one band-aid.

pictures fly by too quickly:
scenes of blood and glory,
death and desolation,
frustration's desire,
the elation of a child
and their wonder.

Sinking down brings me up
fat bass drifting to the lure
lunch bites back
flashing waters reveal
panic and its rage
life in the moment of struggle
dancing to the art
of self-discovery.

remorse births awareness
of the depths of stress
and strong suggestions
to quit bothering others
and help the step
of those in need –
swift-kicked the asshole,
head high, eyes wide open
starts to truly see
the making of a better me.

-2020-3-12

In respect of the gentleness
Of your spirit, and its fierceness,
Am encouraged to be a
Kinder me.
           Hmmm...

Sounds good. But is it?
           Of course it is.
Provided it comes out of love.
For out of love no one can be
Harmed. Stretched maybe. But
Not harmed.

Boredom any aspect of our being
May express it.

It's not that we have to go to that
Place. It's that we have to
Let this place go.
I don't get bored because I have
Unplumeted depths of being.
I have an infinite aspect
To draw upon (and from).
My brain has to become tired of
trying to control everything (act this way because it worked in the
past)
And then the deeper self surfaces.
And if we get far enough into it...
The spirit speaks.

     -20-3-12

this is not a love poem.

an apple grew next to some
          rhubarb.
the rhubarb grew next to
                    the garlic,
which kept the beetles from
          the potatoes.

catnip loves bees who
          love her back.

but bees are busy
          one flower does not make
                    the hour...
          but they must kiss the sweetness
                    from a million lips
          before they shuffle into
                    stillness.

no bee am i.
          one womyn has a million
kisses to give.

i would try each and everyone...

          before i pass...

                    onto another...

if i have time
and the inclination.

          -20-3-14

prisoner's poet

mad monk of the abbey

cut the stone with edict
        and opinion.

it will not matter.
        they cannot mend the broken
                matters of the heart.

they sit in prayer & meditation.

invest themselves in contemplation

        and fight the growing awareness
that the opportunities being
                missed...

are the lives of thousands
        being enriched
                with understanding,
and strengthened in awareness
        of how to live with
                peace
                        within

and without.

        -20-3-14

for you are the birth of an idea,
       the spark that lit the fire
              of creativity.

for you are the gift creation gave
       itself.

you are a figment of creator's
                 imagination.

look what you do
       with it.

listen to the voices with which
              we speak.

       to ourselves.
       to each other.

you do not have a beginning
       and an end.
              what a sill lie we let
                 others tell us.

you contain the infinite.
       you are sprung from
              the fresh of it
       and will be beyond
              its going.

live it.

    -20-3-14

Why have you a peanut in your pocket?

Some kind compulsion has taken hold of you?

Some neurotic desire to maintain constant contact with foodstuffs full of dirt?

Some bizarre rite requiring the appeasement of our earthen goddess?

Some psychotic break permits the peanut a voice within your day?

Speak of what weighs upon your mind that a peanut in the pocket has the answer.

What is this emotion that gives tremolo to your answer?

It is not fear that I hear.

No. I know that quiver. It is the shiver of anticipation.

Tell me. I shall not shout your answer from the rooftops. I simply want to hear.

Why do you have a peanut in your pocket?

Truly? That is all? Show me. I would see this cheeky chipmunk...

This sleek brown fur with racing stripes that bounds with every step.

I would see the creature that evokes such light within your eyes.

Oh wonderful delight!

wouldn't happen to have another peanut on you...

would you?

In Beaver Creek Minimum Security Prison two handfuls of men and a smattering of that most powerful force known to them... womyn... put on a play. A reporter is invited to attend. The players expect a theatrical review. They receive a statement on the impact theatre can have in humanizing prisoners... and a factual report on the criminal history of two of the players. Victims are named.

There are a number of considerations flowing from the situation. Not the least is the expectations of those involved in the play, that the newspaper article would reflect an appraisal of the quality of the players and the production. The severe shock to discover the cold recitation of victims, without consideration for the effect this might have upon the friends and families of the same, appalls the players and those familiar with restorative justice principles, where reflection on the effects of actions is given not only an immediate consideration, but also includes a look toward long-term ramifications and repercussions.

Healing requires a great deal of work. The truth is that many of those who victimize do so because of wounds received themselves. A significant aspect of rehabilitation requires these wounds be addressed. In addressing these wounds, there grows an awareness of the pain negative behaviours causes to others. It is the total of these dynamics that allows people to grow beyond the person that they were.

Anyone who has had to rehabilitate physical disabilities caused by accident or illness knows the pain that can be involved. They also know the long-term commitment required to recover the functions they lost. Now imagine being hurt in such a way, at such an early age, that the person may not have ever had the balance within a function to begin with. For some it isn't a question of recovering what was lost... it is a question of awakening and growing aspects of self not previously known.

Imagine growing sensitive to the hurt within others by addressing the hurt within our self. In growing sensitive to harm, the hardened criminal becomes caring about others as well as themselves. Now imagine that victims decades old are resurrected and bludgeoned again with brutal facts. In this way, victimizers grown beyond harmful behaviours are used by others to cause pain once again to people the victimizers deeply regret having harmed in the first place. This is one truth within the recitation of historical facts.

Socially we once laughed and made jokes of the sensitive new age man. But the natural outgrowth of people like Mother Theresa, Mahatma Ghandi, Martin Luther King, Malcolm X, Cat Stevens, John Lennon, Pete Seiger, and thousands of others... is movements like the open ear now being directed to sexual abuse within the workplace. Why not reawaken the power of theatre to humanize our human condition from new-old understandings of intrinsic values and worth? The play at the centre of the recent splash within the pool of consciousness of some speaks to how easily we can become lost in the life we create for ourselves.

We are all cast into this life together in this moment in time and space. The Titanic is sinking for those blindly abusing without awareness. Take to the lifeboats. Help one another... row. Everyone dies anyway. There's no reason why it has to be alone and afraid.

in the spirit of contented peace,

mighty mouse.

Dear Readers,

Thank you for taking the time to read and enjoy the work of all the talented authors who contributed to this compilation, and for supporting my first poetry publication.

Although my role was simply to compile the poems and publish the end result, it represents a tremendous investment of time and energy. Going into this project, I initially thought it would take less than a week to complete - turning it from handwritten poetry into its present digital format. I was so wrong. I want to thank all of my friends and family who helped me edit, format, and put the finishing touches on this book. I also want to thank all the men who expressed their innermost thoughts and experiences in the beautiful poetry within these pages.

From the book's inception, I had planned for it to be a standalone work. However, I find myself so proud of what we've done here that I would love for the series to continue. My hope is that you feel the same way. If you want more Penitentiary Poetry, please spread the word. Tell your family and friends about this book, tell your coworkers, even your barista. Please follow us on social media *@pentuppoems* and share your thoughts and reviews too (Amazon reviews are always appreciated)!

Until next time,

- Cory Kaufmann

Donations:
@pentuppoems

101

Manufactured by Amazon.ca
Bolton, ON